The Way of the Cross with the Carmelite Saints

Compiled and illustrated by
Sister Joseph Marie of the Trinity, C.H.T.
Carmelite Hermit of the Trinity

About the Editor

Sister Joseph Marie of the Trinity, C.H.T., began to live the charism of a canonical Carmelite Hermit of the Trinity in 1982 under a bishop's guidance and made her profession of vows on Holy Trinity Sunday, May 29, 1983. After fifteen years of proven stability in living the hermit vocation, Sister Joseph Marie requested the privilege to live that vocation with the title of "Carmelite." Father General of the Discalced Carmelites, Camilo Maccise O.C.D., formally granted this on July 16, 1997, the solemnity of Our Lady of Mount Carmel. Subsequently the Rule of Life was revised to make it possible for others to live the vocation according to the Rule and charism of a Carmelite Hermit of the Trinity. Anyone interested in the C.H.T. vocation can read more about it on the web at: www.carmelitehermit.org; or write to Sister Joseph Marie c/o ICS Publications.

Sister Joseph Marie has compiled and published a volume of prayer poems called Prayer-Songs (Carmelite Hermit Publications, 2001); she has indexed the volume *The Collected Works of St. John of the Cross* (ICS Publications, 1991); and she has edited two books by Fr. Thomas Dubay, S.M.: *Fire Within* and *Seeking Spiritual Direction*. (*Prayer-Songs* is available through Sister's website and Fr. Dubay's books are available through bookstores everywhere.)

The Way of the Cross with the Carmelite Saints

Compiled and illustrated by
Sister Joseph Marie of the Trinity, C.H.T.
Carmelite Hermit of the Trinity

ICS Publications
Institute of Carmelite Studies
Washington, D.C.
2003

ICS Publications
2131 Lincoln Road NE
Washington, DC 20002-1199
800-832-8489
www.icspublications.org

*Typeset by Stephen Tiano Page Design & Production
and produced in the U.S.A.*

Library of Congress Cataloging-in-Publication Data

The way of the Cross with the Carmelite saints / compiled and
illustrated by Sister Joseph Marie of the Trinity.
    p. cm.
Includes bibliographical references.
    ISBN 0-935216-29-4
1. Stations of the Cross. I. Joseph Marie, Sister, 1944– .
BX2040.W35 2002
232.96--dc21

2002010259

Contents

THE WAY OF THE CROSS
with Saint John of the Cross

Because I have said that Christ is the way and that this way is a death to our natural selves … , I would like to demonstrate how this death is patterned on Christ's, for He is our model and light.*

I
JESUS IS CONDEMNED TO DEATH

They all concurred in the verdict guilty, with its
sentence of death (Mark 14:64).

Take neither great nor little notice of who is with you or against
you, and try always to please God. Ask Him that His Will be
done in you. Love Him intensely, as He deserves to be loved.[1]

... Have a great love for those who contradict and fail to love
you, for in this way love is begotten in a heart that has no love.
God so acts with us. ... [2]

When something distasteful or unpleasant comes your way,
remember Christ crucified and be silent.[3]

II
JESUS CARRIES HIS CROSS

Jesus was led away ... carrying the cross
by Himself (John 19:16-17).

He who seeks not the cross of Christ seeks not the glory of Christ.[4]

... It behooves us not to go without the cross, just as our Beloved did not go without it, even to the death of love ... .[5]

Oh! If we could but now fully understand how a soul cannot reach the thicket and wisdom of the riches of God, which are of many kinds, without entering the thicket of many kinds of suffering, finding in this her delight and consolation; and how a soul with an authentic desire for divine wisdom, wants suffering first in order to enter this wisdom by the thicket of the cross![6]

III
JESUS FALLS THE FIRST TIME

**I was hard pressed and was falling
(Psalm 118:13).**

On this [narrow] road there is room only for self-denial (as our Savior asserts) and the cross. The cross is a supporting staff and greatly lightens and eases the journey.[7]

... Not only are temporal goods and bodily delights contradictory to the path leading to God, but so also are spiritual consolations, if possessed or sought with attachment, an obstacle to the way of the cross of Christ, the Bridegroom.[8]

IV
JESUS MEETS HIS AFFLICTED
MOTHER

Simeon said to Mary His mother ... you yourself
shall be pierced with a sword (Luke 2:34-35).

Sometimes, however, and at certain periods, God allows [the soul]
to feel things and suffer from them that she might gain more merit
and grow in the fervor of love, or for other reasons, as He did with
the Virgin Mother, St. Paul, and others.[9]

V
SIMON OF CYRENE HELPS JESUS CARRY HIS CROSS

They pressed [Simon] into service to carry the
Cross (Mark 15:21).

Our Lord proclaimed through St. Matthew: My yoke is sweet and my burden light [Mt. 11:30], the burden being the cross. If individuals resolutely submit to the carrying of the cross, if they decidedly want to find and endure trial in all things for God, they will discover in all of them great relief and sweetness.[10]

Some souls obtain sensible or spiritual sweetness from God because they are incapable of eating the stronger and more solid food of the trials of the cross of His Son. He would desire them to take the cross more than any other thing.[11]

VI
VERONICA WIPES THE FACE OF JESUS

There was in Him no stately bearing to make us
look at Him (Is. 53:2).

When there is union of love, the image of the Beloved is so sketched in the will, and drawn so intimately and vividly, that it is true to say that the Beloved lives in the lover and the lover in the Beloved ... . Everything can be called a sketch of love in comparison with that perfect image, the transformation in glory. Yet the attainment of such a sketch of transformation in this life is a great blessing, for with this transformation the Beloved is very pleased. Desiring the bride to put Him as a sketch in her soul, He said in the Song of Songs: *Put Me as a seal upon your heart ...* [Sg. 8:6].[12]

To the soul that is more advanced in love, more conformed to the divine Will, God communicates Himself more. A person who has reached complete conformity and likeness of will has attained total supernatural union and transformation in God.[13]

8

VII
JESUS FALLS THE SECOND TIME

My strength has failed through affliction
(Psalm 31:11).

Since you walk in these darknesses and voids of spiritual poverty, you think that everyone and everything is failing you. It is no wonder that in this it also seems God is failing you. But nothing is failing you ... . Those who desire nothing else than God walk not in darkness, however poor and dark they are in their own sight. And those who walk not presumptuously, nor according to their own satisfactions, whether from God or from creatures, nor do their own will in anything, have nothing to stumble over ... [14]

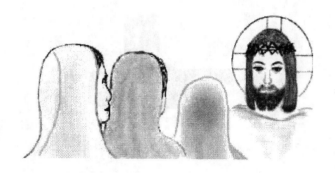

VIII
JESUS MEETS THE WOMEN OF JERUSALEM

Do not weep for Me. Weep for yourselves and for
your children (Luke 23:28).

... Christ is little known by those who consider themselves His
friends. For we see them going about seeking in Him their own
consolations and satisfactions, loving themselves very much, but
not loving Him very much by seeking His bitter trials and
deaths.[15]

IX
JESUS FALLS A THIRD TIME

I looked about, but there was no one to help ... no
one to lend support (Is. 63:5).

If you do not fear falling alone, do you presume that you will rise
up alone? Consider how much more can be accomplished by two
together than by one alone.[16]

X
JESUS IS STRIPPED OF HIS GARMENTS

They divided His clothes among them
(Mt. 27:35).

… The soul that is naked of desires and whims, God will clothe with His purity, pleasure, and will.[17]

Wishing to strip them in fact of this old self and clothe them with the new, which is created according to God … as the Apostle says [Col. 3:9-10; Eph. 4:22-24; Rom. 12:2], God divests the faculties, affections, and senses, both spiritual and sensory, interior and exterior. He leaves the intellect in darkness, the will in aridity, the memory in emptiness, and the affections in supreme affliction, bitterness and anguish by depriving the soul of the feeling and satisfaction it previously obtained from spiritual blessings. For this privation is one of the conditions required that the spiritual form, which is the union of love, may be introduced into the spirit and united with it.[18]

XI
JESUS IS NAILED TO THE CROSS

They have pierced my hands and feet
(Psalm 22:17).

Crucified inwardly and outwardly with Christ, you will live in this life with fullness and satisfaction of soul, and possess your soul in patience [Luke 21:19].[19]

Let Christ crucified be enough for you, and with Him suffer and take your rest, and hence annihilate yourself in all inward and outward things.[20]

XII
JESUS DIES ON THE CROSS

Through his suffering, my servant shall justify many
... he surrendered himself to death (Is. 53:11-12).

... He brought about the reconciliation and union of the human race with God through grace. The Lord achieved this ... at the moment in which He was most annihilated in all things: in His reputation before people ... ; in His human nature, by dying; and in spiritual help and consolation from His Father, for He was forsaken. ... The journey, then, does not consist in consolations, delights, and spiritual feelings, but in the living death of the cross, sensory and spiritual, exterior and interior.[21]

True love receives all things that come from the Beloved — prosperity, adversity, even chastisement — with the same evenness of soul, since they are His Will ... Death cannot be bitter to the soul that loves, for in it she finds all the sweetness and delight of love ... . She thinks of death as her friend and bridegroom, and at the thought of it she rejoices as she would over the thought of her betrothal and marriage, and she longs for that day and that hour of her death ... [22]

XIII
JESUS IS TAKEN DOWN FROM THE CROSS

They came and took the body away
(John 19:38).

However intimate may be a person's union with God, there will never be satisfaction and rest until God's glory appears [Ps. 17:15] ... [23]

It is vital for individuals to make acts of love in this life so that in being perfected in a short time they may not be detained long, either here on earth or in the next life, before seeing God.[24]

XIV
JESUS IS LAID IN THE TOMB

... but when they entered the tomb, they did not
find the body of the Lord Jesus (Luke 24:3).

If you desire to be perfect, sell your will, give it to the poor in
spirit, come to Christ in meekness and humility, and follow Him
to Calvary and the sepulcher.[25]

It is fitting that the soul be in this sepulcher of dark death in
order that it attain the spiritual resurrection for which it hopes.[26]

JESUS IS RISEN
ETERNAL LIFE:
UNION WITH THE HOLY TRINITY

Oh, what blessings we will enjoy in the vision of the Most Blessed Trinity![27]

Notes

Quotations are from *The Collected Works of St. John of the Cross*, trans. Kieran Kavanaugh and Otilio Rodriguez (Washington, DC: ICS Publications, 1991).

* Introductory quote: *The Ascent of Mount Carmel*, Bk. II, ch. 7, no. 9, p. 172.

1. *The Sayings of Light and Love*, no. 155, p. 96.
2. *The Letters*, no. 33, p. 764.
3. *Letters*, no. 20, p. 756.
4. *Sayings*, no. 102, p. 92.
5. *Letters*, no. 11, p. 745.
6. *The Spiritual Canticle*, stanza 36, no. 13, p. 614.
7. *Ascent*, Bk. II, ch. 7, no. 7, p. 171.
8. *Canticle*, stanza 3, no. 5, p. 492.
9. *Ibid.*, stanzas 20 & 21, no. 10, p. 556.
10. *Ascent*, Bk. II, ch. 7, no. 7, p. 171.
11. *Ibid.*, Bk. II, ch. 21, no. 3, p. 224.
12. *Canticle*, stanza 12, nos. 7-8, pp. 517-18.
13. *Ascent*, Bk. II, ch. 5, no. 4, pp. 163-64.
14. *Letters*, no. 19, p. 754.
15. *Ascent*, Bk. II, ch. 7, no. 12, p. 173
16. *Sayings*, no. 9, p. 86.
17. *Ibid.*, no. 98, p. 92.
18. *The Dark Night*, Bk. II, ch. 3, no, 3, p. 399.
19. *Sayings*, no. 87, p. 92.
20. *Ibid.*, no. 92, p. 92.
21. *Ascent*, Bk. II, ch. 7, no. 11, p. 172.
22. *Canticle*, Stanza 11, no. 10, p. 513.
23. *The Living Flame of Love*, stanza 1, no. 27, p. 652.
24. *Ibid.*, stanza 1, no. 34, p. 656.
25. *Sayings*, no. 165, p. 97.
26. *Dark Night*, Bk. II, ch. 6, no. 1, p. 404.
27. *Sayings*, no. 172, p. 97.

THE WAY OF THE CROSS
with Saint Teresa of Avila

He showed me His wounds in order to encourage me when I was suffering tribulation. Sometimes He appeared on the cross or in the garden, and a few times with the crown of thorns; sometimes He also appeared carrying the cross ... But His body was always glorified.*

I
JESUS IS CONDEMNED TO DEATH

They all concurred in the verdict guilty, with its
sentence of death (Mark 14:64).

When the soul reaches the stage at which it pays little attention to
praise, it pays much less to disapproval; on the contrary, it rejoices
in this... This is an amazing truth. Blame does not intimidate the
soul but strengthens it ... . And since it clearly experiences the
benefits of persecution, it acquires a special and very tender love
for its persecutors. It seems to it that they are greater friends and
more advantageous than those who speak well of it.[1]

I ask you why,
Him they condemn?
Innocent He is,
And without evil.[2]

II
JESUS CARRIES HIS CROSS

Jesus was led away ... carrying the Cross
by Himself (John 19:16-17).

They are too attached to their honor .... These souls, for the most part, grieve over anything said against them. They do not embrace the cross but drag it along, and so it hurts and wearies them and breaks them to pieces. However, if the cross is loved, it is easy to bear; this is certain.[3]

He wants to lead you as though you were strong, giving you the cross here below, something that His Majesty always had. What better friendship than that He desire for you what He desired for Himself?[4]

III
JESUS FALLS THE FIRST TIME

I was hard pressed and was falling
(Psalm 118:13).

I don't see, Lord, nor do I know how the road that leads to You is narrow [cf. Mk. 10:28]. I see that it is a royal road, not a path; a road that is safer for anyone who indeed takes it. Very far off are the occasions of sin, those narrow mountain passes and the rocks that make one fall. What I would call a path, a wretched path and a narrow way, is the kind which has on one side, where a soul can fall, a valley far below, and on the other side a precipice ... . He who really loves You, my Good, walks safely on a broad and royal road and is far from the precipice. Hardly has he begun to stumble when You, Lord, give him Your hand. One fall is not sufficient for a person to be lost, nor are many, if he loves You and not the things of the world. He journeys in the valley of humility.[5]

IV
JESUS MEETS HIS AFFLICTED MOTHER

Simeon said to Mary His mother ... you yourself
shall be pierced with a sword (Luke 2:34-35).

He did not complain. Nor did He do so when in the prayer of the
garden He went to awaken His apostles. With greater reason might
He have complained to His Mother and our Lady when she was
at the foot of the cross, and not asleep but suffering in her most
holy soul and dying a harsh death; it always consoles us more to
complain to those who we know feel our trials and love us more.[6]

We have always seen that those who were closest to Christ our
Lord were those with the greatest trials. Let us look at what His
glorious Mother suffered.[7]

V
SIMON OF CYRENE HELPS JESUS
CARRY HIS CROSS

They pressed [Simon] into service to carry the
cross (Mark 15:21).

Embracing the cross,
Let us follow Jesus;
He is our way and light
Abounding in consolations.[8]

All bear their crosses even though these crosses be different. For
all who follow Christ, if they don't want to get lost, must walk
along this path that He trod.[9]

If a person wishes to gain freedom of spirit and not be always
troubled, let him begin by not being frightened by the cross, and
he will see how the Lord also helps him carry it. ... [10]

VI
VERONICA WIPES THE FACE OF JESUS

There was in Him no stately bearing to make us
look at Him (Is. 53:2).

If you are experiencing trials or are sad, ... behold Him burdened
with the cross, ... He will look at you with those eyes so beautiful and compassionate, filled with tears; He will forget His sorrows
so as to console you in yours, merely because you yourselves go
to Him to be consoled, and you turn your head to look at Him.[11]

VII
JESUS FALLS THE SECOND TIME

My strength has failed through affliction
(Psalm 31:11).

In stumbling, in falling with [Christ], do not withdraw from the cross or abandon it. Consider carefully the fatigue with which He walks and how much greater His trials are than those trials you suffer, however great you may want to paint them and no matter how much you grieve over them.[12]

Contemplatives ... must keep the flag of humility raised and suffer all the blows they receive without returning any. Their duty is to suffer as Christ did, to hold high the cross, not to let it out of their hand whatever the dangers they see themselves in ... . for if he lets go of the flag the battle will be lost.[13]

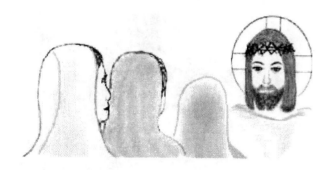

VIII
JESUS MEETS THE WOMEN OF JERUSALEM

Do not weep for Me. Weep for yourselves and for
your children (Luke 23:28).

Why must we want so many blessings and delights and so much
endless glory all at the cost of the good Jesus? Shall we not at
least weep with the daughters of Jerusalem since we do not, with
the Cyrenian, help Him carry His cross?[14]

The Lord told me this: ... "Behold these wounds, for your sufferings have never reached this point. Suffering is the way of truth.
By this means you will help me weep over the loss of those who
follow the way of the world ... "[15]

IX
JESUS FALLS A THIRD TIME

I looked about, but there was no one to help ...
no one to lend support (Is. 63:5).

So I have experience that the true remedy against a fall is to be
attached to the cross and trust in Him who placed Himself on it.[16]

> This sacred cross,
> An olive tree so dear,
> With its oil anoints us
> Giving us light.
> My soul, take up this cross
> Rich with consolations great.
> It alone is the road
> Leading to Heaven.[17]

X
JESUS IS STRIPPED OF HIS GARMENTS

They divided His clothes among them
(Mt. 27:35).

It seems I've forgotten Your grandeurs and mercies and how You've come into the world of sinners and have purchased us for so great a price and have paid for our false joys by suffering such cruel torments and blows. You have cured my blindness with the blindfold that covered Your divine eyes and my vanity with that cruel crown of thorns![18]

Who is it that sees the Lord covered with wounds and afflicted with persecutions who will not embrace them, love them, and desire them?[19]

XI
JESUS IS NAILED TO THE CROSS

They have pierced my hands and feet
(Psalm 22:17).

Fix yours eyes on the Crucified and everything will become small
for you. If His Majesty showed us His love by means of such works
and frightful torments, how is it you want to please Him only with
words? Do you know what it means to be truly spiritual? It means
becoming the slaves of God. Marked with His brand, which is
that of the cross, ... [20]

> After our Savior
> Upon the cross placed Himself,
> Now in this cross is
> Both glory and honor.
> In suffering pain
> There is life and comfort,
> And the safest road
> Leading to heaven.[21]

XII
JESUS DIES ON THE CROSS

Through his suffering, my servant shall justify
many ... he surrendered himself to death
(Is. 53:11-12).

"Your will be done on earth as it is in heaven"... Well, I want to advise you and remind you what His will is. Don't fear that it means He will give you riches, or delights, or honors, or all these earthly things. His love for you is not that small .... Do you want to know how He answers those who say these words to Him sincerely? Ask His glorious Son, who said them while praying in the Garden. .... See if the Father's will wasn't done fully in Him through the trials, sorrows, injuries, and persecutions He suffered until His life came to an end through death on a cross.

Well, see here ... what He gave to the one He loved most. By that we understand what His will is. For these are His gifts in this world. He gives according to the love He bears us .... And He gives according to the courage He sees in each ... He will see that whoever loves Him much will be able to suffer much for Him; whoever loves Him little will be capable of little ... The measure for being able to bear a large or small cross is love.[22]

XIII
JESUS IS TAKEN DOWN FROM THE CROSS

They came and took the body away
(Jn. 19:38).

Whoever doesn't want to use a little effort now to recollect at least the sense of sight and look at this Lord within herself ... would have been much less able to stay at the foot of the cross with the Magdalene, who saw His death with her own eyes. But how much the glorious Virgin and this blessed saint must have suffered! How many threats, how many wicked words, how much shoving about and rudeness! ... Indeed what these two suffered must have been terrible; but in the presence of another greater affliction they didn't feel their own.[23]

XIV
JESUS IS LAID IN THE TOMB

... but when they entered the tomb, they did not
find the body of the Lord Jesus (Luke 24:3).

> Calvary or Tabor give me,
> Desert or fruitful land;
> As Job in suffering
> Or John at Your breast;
> Barren or fruitful vine,
> Whatever be Your will:
> What do You want of me?[24]

Now is the time to take what this compassionate Lord and God of
ours gives us. Since He desires our friendship, who will deny it
to one who did not refuse to shed all His blood and lose His life
for us? Behold that what He asks for is nothing, since giving it is
for our own benefit.[25]

36

JESUS IS RISEN
ETERNAL LIFE:
UNION WITH THE HOLY TRINITY

Look at Him as risen. Just imagining how He rose from the tomb will bring you joy. The brilliance! The beauty! The Majesty! How victorious! How joyful! Indeed, like one coming forth from a battle where He has gained a great kingdom! And all of that, plus Himself, He desires for you.[26]

If our nature or health doesn't allow us to think always about the Passion, since to do so would be arduous, who will prevent us from being with Him in His risen state? We have Him so near in the Blessed Sacrament, where He is already glorified and where we don't have to gaze upon Him as being so tired and worn out, bleeding, wearied by His journeys, persecuted by those for whom He did so much good … Certainly there is no one who can endure thinking all the time about the many trials He suffered. Behold Him here without suffering, full of glory … our companion in the most Blessed Sacrament.[27]

Notes

Quotations are from *The Collected Works of St. Teresa of Avila*, trans. Kieran Kavanaugh and Otilio Rodriguez, 3 vols. (Washington, DC: ICS Publications, 1976-85).

* Introductory quote: *The Collected Works*, vol. one, *The Book of Her Life*, ch. 29, no. 4, pp. 189-90.
1. The Complete Works, vol. two, *The Interior Castle: The Sixth Dwelling Places*, ch. 1, no. 5, pp. 361-62.
2. *Ibid.*, vol. three, *Minor Works: Poetry*, trans. Adrian J. Cooney, O.C.D.; no. 15, "The Circumcision," p. 391.
3. *Ibid.*, vol. two, *Meditations on the Song of Songs*, ch. 2, no. 26, p. 234.
4. *Ibid.*, *The Way of Perfection*, ch. 17, no. 7, p. 101.
5. *Ibid.*, vol. one, *Life*, ch. 35, nos. 13-14, pp. 239-40.
6. *Ibid.*, vol. two, *Meditations*, ch. 3, no. 11, p. 241.
7. *Ibid.*, *Interior Castle: The Seventh Dwelling Places*, ch. 4, no. 5, p. 445.
8. *Ibid.*, vol. three, *Poetry*, no. 20, "Embracing the Cross," p. 396.
9. *Ibid.*, vol. one, *Life*, ch. 11, no. 5, p. 80.
10. *Ibid.*, no. 17, p. 85.
11. *Ibid.*, vol. two, *Way*, ch. 26, no. 5, pp. 134-35.
12. *Ibid.*, no. 7, p. 135.
13. *Ibid.*, ch. 18, no. 5, p. 104.
14. *Ibid.*, vol. one, *Life*, ch. 27, no. 13, p. 178.
15. *Ibid.*, *Spiritual Testimonies*, no. 32: 1, pp. 336-37.
16. *Ibid.*, no. 3:1, p. 319.
17. *Ibid.*, vol. three, *Poetry*, no. 19, "The Way of the Cross," p. 395.
18. *Ibid.*, vol. one, *Soliloquies: III*, no. 3, p. 377.
19. *Ibid.*, *Life*, ch.2, no. 5, p. 173.
20. *Ibid.*, vol. two, *Interior Castle: The Seventh Dwelling Places*, ch. 4, no. 8, p.446.
21. *Ibid.*, vol. three, *Poetry*, no. 19, "The Way of the Cross," p. 396.
22. *Ibid.*, Way, ch. 32, nos. 2, 6-7, pp. 160-62.

23. *Ibid.*, ch. 26, no. 8, pp. 135-36.
24. *Ibid.*, vol. three, *Poetry*, no. 2, "In the Hands of God," pp. 378-79.
25. *Ibid.*, vol. one, *Soliloquies: XIV*, no. 3, p. 387.
26. *Ibid.*, vol. two, *Way*, ch. 26, no. 4, p. 134.
27. *Ibid.*, vol. one, *Life*, ch. 22, no. 6, p. 146.

THE WAY OF THE CROSS
with Saint Thérèse of the Child Jesus

The little flower transplanted to Mount Carmel was to expand under the shadow of the cross. The tears and blood of Jesus were to be her dew, and her Sun was His adorable Face veiled with tears... I understood what real glory was. He whose Kingdom is not of this world showed me that true wisdom consists in "desiring to be unknown and counted as nothing."*

I
JESUS IS CONDEMNED TO DEATH

They all concurred in the verdict guilty, with its
sentence of death (Mark 14:64).

I've never acted like Pilate, who refused to listen to the truth. I've
always said to God: O my God, I really want to listen to You; I beg
You to answer me when I say humbly: What is truth? Make me see
things as they really are. Let nothing cause me to be deceived.[1]

What is our humiliation at the moment is our glory later on,
even in this life.[2]

It was night! The dark night of the soul! I felt I was all alone in
the garden of Gethsemani like Jesus, and I found no consolation on
earth or from heaven; God Himself seemed to have abandoned me.[3]

II
JESUS CARRIES HIS CROSS

Jesus was led away ... carrying the cross
by Himself (John 19:16-17).

[St. Teresa of Avila] said that to souls whom God loves with an
ordinary love He gives some trials, but on those He loves with a
love of predilection He lavishes His crosses as the most certain
mark of His tenderness.[4]

Yes, ... Jesus is there with His cross! Privileged one of His
love, He wills to make you like Him! Why be frightened at not
being able to carry this cross without weakening?[5]

It is getting late, the day is now far spent.
Come guide me, Lord, on the way.
With Your cross, I'm scaling the hill,
Stay with me, Heavenly Pilgrim ... .[6]

III
JESUS FALLS THE FIRST TIME

I was hard pressed and was falling
(Psalm 118:13).

To be little is not attributing to oneself the virtues that one practices, believing oneself capable of anything, but to recognize that God places this treasure in the hands of His little child to be used when necessary; but it remains always God's treasure. Finally, it is not to become discouraged over one's faults, for children fall often, but they are too little to hurt themselves much.[7]

> But if I fall with each passing hour,
> You come to my aid, lifting me up.
> At each moment You give me Your grace:
> I live on Love.[8]

IV
JESUS MEETS HIS AFFLICTED
MOTHER

Simeon said to Mary His mother ... you yourself
shall be pierced with a sword (Luke 2:34-35).

O Queen of martyrs, till the evening of your life
That sorrowful sword will pierce your heart.[9]

Mary, at the top of Calvary standing beside the cross
To me you seem like a priest at the altar,
Offering your beloved Jesus ... .
A prophet said, O afflicted Mother,
"There is no sorrow like your sorrow!"[10]

V

SIMON OF CYRENE HELPS JESUS CARRY HIS CROSS

They pressed [Simon] into service to carry the cross (Mark 15:21).

I have come to sing the inexpressible grace
Of having suffered ... of having borne the cross ...
For a long time I have drunk from the chalice of tears.
I have shared Your cup of sorrows,
And I have understood that suffering has its charms,
That by the cross we save sinners.[11]

Living on Love is not setting up one's tent
At the top of Tabor.
It's climbing Calvary with Jesus,
It's looking at the cross as a treasure! ...
In Heaven I'm to live on joy,
Then trials will have fled forever,
But in exile, in suffering I want
To live on Love.[12]

VI
VERONICA WIPES THE FACE OF JESUS

There was in Him no stately bearing to make us
look at Him (Is. 53:2).

My love discovers the charms
Of Your Face adorned with tears.
I smile through my own tears
When I contemplate Your sorrows ... .
Your beauty, which You know how to veil,
Discloses for me all its mystery ... .
Leave in me the Divine impress
Of Your Features ... .[13]

These words of Isaias: "Who has believed our report?... There is
no beauty in Him, no comeliness, etc.," have made the whole foundation of my devotion to the Holy Face, or, to express it better,
the foundation of all my piety. I, too, have desired to be without
beauty, alone in treading the winepress, unknown to everyone.[14]

VII
JESUS FALLS THE SECOND TIME

My strength has failed through affliction
(Psalm 31:11).

We'd never want to fall?... What does it matter, my Jesus, if I fall at each moment; I see my weakness through this and this is a great gain for me.[15]

I never cease to say to God: "O my God, I beg You, preserve me from the misfortune of being unfaithful." ... For example, if I were to say to myself: I have acquired a certain virtue, and I am certain I can practice it ... This would be relying upon my own strength, and when we do this, we run the risk of falling into the abyss. However, I will have the right of doing stupid things up until my death, if I am humble and if I remain little. Look at little children: they never stop breaking things, tearing things, falling down ... . When I fall in this way, it makes me realize my nothingness more.[16]

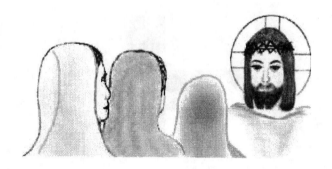

VIII
JESUS MEETS THE WOMEN OF JERUSALEM

Do not weep for Me. Weep for yourselves and for your children (Luke 23:28).

Women, how they are misunderstood! And yet they love God in much larger numbers than men do and during the Passion of Our Lord, women had more courage than the apostles since they braved the insults of the soldiers and dared to dry the adorable Face of Jesus. It is undoubtedly because of this that He allows misunderstanding to be their lot on earth, since He chose it for Himself.[17]

My first steps met with more thorns than roses! Yes, suffering opened wide its arms to me and I threw myself into them with love.[18]

IX
JESUS FALLS A THIRD TIME

I looked about, but there was no one to help ...
no one to lend support (Is. 63:5).

Jesus on the road to Calvary fell three times, and, you .... you would
not be willing to fall a hundred times if necessary to prove your
love for Him, rising with greater strength than before your fall![19]

Yes, I'm like a tired and harassed traveler, who reaches the end
of his journey and falls over. Yes, but I'll be falling into God's arms![20]

I understand very well why St. Peter fell. Poor Peter, he was
relying upon himself instead of relying only upon God's strength ...
Before Peter fell, Our Lord had said to him: "And once you are con-
verted, strengthen your brethren." This means: Convince them of
the weakness of human strength through your own experience.[21]

X
JESUS IS STRIPPED OF HIS GARMENTS

They divided His clothes among them
(Mt. 27:35).

The poor in spirit follow Jesus' counsel: "If anyone take away your coat, let go your cloak also" [Mt. 5:40]. To give up one's cloak is, it seems to me, renouncing one's ultimate rights; it is considering oneself as the servant and the slave of others. When one has left his cloak, it is much easier to walk, to run, and Jesus adds: "and whoever forces you to go one mile, go two more with Him" [Mt. 5:41].[22]

My intention is not to give My beloved her homeland, her titles, and her riches now. I will that she share the lot it pleased Me to choose on earth ... . I will that she hide the gifts she has received from Me, allowing Me to give them to her or take them back, just as I please, not attaching herself to a single one.[23]

XI
JESUS IS NAILED TO THE CROSS

They have pierced my hands and feet
(Psalm 22:17).

Looking at a picture of Our Lord on the cross, I was struck by the blood flowing from one of the divine hands. I felt a great pang of sorrow when thinking this blood was falling to the ground without anyone's hastening to gather it up. I was resolved to remain in spirit at the foot of the cross and to receive the divine dew. I understood I was then to pour it out upon souls. The cry of Jesus on the cross sounded continually in my heart: "I thirst!" These words ignited within me an unknown and very living fire. I wanted to give my Beloved to drink and I felt myself consumed with a thirst for souls.[24]

XII
JESUS DIES ON THE CROSS

Through his suffering, my servant shall justify
many ... he surrendered himself to death
(Is. 53:11-12).

Yes, it is painful to be looked at and laughed at when one is suffering. But I think how Our Lord on the cross was looked at in the same way in the midst of His suffering. It was even worse, for they were really mocking Him; isn't it said in the Gospels that they looked at Him, shaking their heads? This thought aids me in offering Him this sacrifice in the right spirit.[25]

Our Lord died on the cross in agony and yet this is the most beautiful death of love. ... To die of love is not to die in transports.[26]

I am not sorry for delivering myself up to Love.[27]

XIII
JESUS IS TAKEN DOWN FROM THE CROSS

They came and took the body away
(Jn. 19:38).

The Blessed Virgin Mary held her dead Jesus on her knees, and He was disfigured, covered with blood! ... Ah! I don't know how she stood it![28]

> You love us, Mary, as Jesus loves us ... .
> Refuge of sinners, He leaves us to you
> When He leaves the cross to wait for us in Heaven.[29]

See then, all that Jesus lays claim to from us: He has no need of our works, but only of our love ... . Jesus is parched, for He meets only the ungrateful and indifferent among His disciples in the world, and among His own disciples, alas, He finds few hearts who surrender to Him without reservations, who understand the real tenderness of His infinite Love.[30]

XIV
JESUS IS LAID IN THE TOMB

... but when they entered the tomb, they did not find the body of the Lord Jesus (Luke 24:3).

At the Holy Sepulchre, Mary Magdalene,
Searching for her Jesus, stooped down in tears.
The angels wanted to console her sorrow,
But nothing could calm her grief … .
She wanted to see the Lord of the Angels,
To take Him in her arms, to carry Him far away.

Close by the tomb, the last one to stay,
She had come well before dawn.
Her God also came … .[31]

Just as Mary Magdalene found what she was seeking by always stooping down and looking into the empty tomb, so I, abasing myself to the very depths of my nothingness, raised myself so high that I was able to attain my end.[32]

JESUS IS RISEN
ETERNAL LIFE:
UNION WITH THE HOLY TRINITY

I thank you, O my God! for all the graces You have granted me, especially the grace of making me pass through the crucible of suffering. It is with joy I shall contemplate You on the Last Day carrying the scepter of Your cross. Since You deigned to give me a share in this very precious cross, I hope in heaven to resemble You and to see shining in my glorified body the sacred stigmata of Your Passion.[33]

Coming into this land of exile, You willed to suffer and to die in order to draw souls to the bosom of the Eternal Fire of the Blessed Trinity. Ascending once again to the Inaccessible Light, henceforth Your abode, You remain still in this "valley of tears," hidden beneath the appearances of a white Host.[34]

I've found my Heaven in the Blessed Trinity.[35]

Notes

Quotations are from *St. Thérèse of Lisieux: General Correspondence,* trans. John Clarke, 2 vols. (Washington, DC: ICS Publications, 1982-88); *St. Thérèse of Lisieux: Her Last Conversations,* trans. John Clarke (Washington, DC: ICS Publications, 1977); *Story of a Soul: The Autobiography of Saint Thérèse of Lisieux* (Washington, DC: ICS Publications, 1976); *The Poetry of Saint Thérèse of Lisieux,* trans. Donald Kinney (Washington, DC: ICS Publications,1995).

* Introductory quote: *Story of a Soul: The Autobiography of St. Thérèse,* ch. VII, pp. 151-52.

1. *St. Thérèse of Lisieux: Her Last Conversations,* The "Yellow Notebook" of Mother Agnes, July 21, no. 4, p. 105.

2. *Ibid.,* July 29, no. 13, p. 117.

3. *Story,* ch. 5, p. 109.

4. *St. Thérèse of Lisieux: General Correspondence,* vol. two; LT 178, p. 909.

5. *Ibid.,* vol. one; LT 81, p. 529.

6. *The Poetry of St. Thérèse of Lisieux,* PN 31: 2, p. 150.

7. *Conversations: Notebook,* Aug. 6, no. 8, p. 139.

8. *Poetry,* PN 17: 7, p. 91.

9. *Ibid.,* PN 54: 12, p. 217.

10. *Ibid.,* PN 54: 23, p. 220.

11. *Ibid.,* PN 16: 1-2, p. 85.

12. *Ibid.,* PN 17: 4, p. 90.

13. *Ibid.,* PN 20: 1,2, 5; pp. 109-10.

14. *Conversations: Notebook,* Aug. 5, no. 9, p. 135.

15. *Correspondence,* vol. one; LT 89, p. 557.

16. *Conversations: Notebook,* Aug. 7, no. 4, p. 140.

17. *Story,* ch. VI, p. 140.

18. *Ibid.,* ch. VII, p. 149.

19. *Correspondence,* vol. one; LT 81, p. 529.

20. *Conversations: Notebook,* Sept. 15, no. 2, p. 191.

21. *Ibid.*, Aug. 7, no. 4, pp. 140-41.
22. *Story*, ch. X, pp. 226-27.
23. *Correspondence*, vol. two; LT 183, p. 933.
24. *Story*, ch. V, p. 99.
25. *Conversations: Notebook*, Aug. 25, no. 1, p. 167.
26. *Ibid.*, July 4, no. 2, p. 73.
27. *Ibid.*, Sept. 30 (the day of her death), p. 205.
28. *Ibid.*, July 25, no. 6, pp. 109-10.
29. *Poetry*, PN 54: 22, p. 219.
30. *Story*, ch. IX, p. 189.
31. *Poetry*, PN 23: 1-2, p. 119.
32. *Story*, ch. IX, p. 194.
33. *Ibid.*, Appendices, Act of Oblation, p. 277.
34. *Ibid.*, ch. IX, p. 199.
35. *Poetry*, PN 32, v. 5, p. 154.

THE WAY OF THE CROSS
with Saint Teresa Benedicta of the Cross

The bridal union of the soul with God is the goal for which she was created, purchased through the cross, consummated on the cross, and sealed for all eternity with the cross.*

I
JESUS IS CONDEMNED TO DEATH

They all concurred in the verdict guilty, with its
sentence of death (Mark 14:64).

When someone desires to suffer, it is not merely a pious reminder
of the suffering of the Lord. Voluntary expiatory suffering is what
truly and really unites one to the Lord intimately. When it arises,
it comes from an already existing relationship with Christ. For,
by nature, a person flees from suffering. And the mania for suffering caused by a perverse lust for pain differs completely from
the desire to suffer in expiation. Such lust is not a spiritual striv-
ing, but a sensory longing no better than other sensory desires; in
fact worse, because it is contrary to nature. Only someone whose
spiritual eyes have been opened to the supernatural correlations
of worldly events can desire suffering in expiation, and this is
only possible for people in whom the Spirit of Christ dwells.[1]

II
JESUS CARRIES HIS CROSS

Jesus was led away ... carrying the cross
by Himself (John 19:16-17).

Everyone who, in the course of time, has borne an onerous destiny in remembrance of the suffering Savior or who has freely taken up works of expiation has by doing so canceled some of the mighty load of human sin and has helped the Lord carry His burden.[2]

More effective than the mortification one practices according to one's own choice is the cross that God lays upon one, exteriorly and interiorly.[3]

Because being one with Christ is our sanctity, and progressively becoming one with Him our happiness on earth, the love of the cross in no way contradicts being a joyful child of God. Helping Christ carry His cross fills one with a strong and pure joy ... [4]

III
JESUS FALLS THE FIRST TIME

I was hard pressed and was falling
(Psalm 118:13).

A *scientia crucis* [knowledge of the cross] can be gained only when one comes to feel the cross radically.[5]

The entire sum of human failures from the first Fall up to the Day of Judgment must be blotted out by a corresponding measure of expiation. The way of the cross is this expiation.[6]

IV
JESUS MEETS HIS AFFLICTED
MOTHER

Simeon said to Mary His mother ... you yourself
shall be pierced with a sword (Luke 2:34-35).

The archetype of followers of the cross for all time is the Mother
of God.[7]

No earthly maternal joy resembles the bliss of a soul permitted
to enkindle the light of grace in the night of sins. The way to this
is the cross. Beneath the cross the Virgin of virgins becomes the
Mother of Grace.[8]

V
SIMON OF CYRENE HELPS JESUS
CARRY HIS CROSS

They pressed [Simon] into service to carry the
cross (Mark 15:21).

Typical of those who submit to the suffering inflicted on them
and experience His blessing by bearing it is Simon of Cyrene.[9]

The followers of Christ have their place in this battle, and
their chief weapon is the cross. What does that mean? The burden of the cross that Christ assumed is that of corrupted human
nature, with all its consequences in sin and suffering to which
fallen humanity is subject. The meaning of the way of the cross
is to carry this burden out of the world.[10]

VI
VERONICA WIPES THE FACE OF JESUS

There was in Him no stately bearing to make us
look at Him (Is. 53:2).

The Savior is not alone on the way of the cross. Not only are there
adversaries around Him who oppress Him but also people who
succor Him .... Representative of those who love Him and yearn
to serve the Lord is Veronica.[11]

I keep having to think of Queen Esther who was taken from
among her people precisely that she might represent them before
the King. I am a very poor and powerless little Esther, but the King
who chose me is infinitely great and merciful.[12]

VII
JESUS FALLS THE SECOND TIME

My strength has failed through affliction
(Psalm 31:11).

We can assume that the prospect of the faithful who would follow Him on His way of the cross strengthened the Savior during
His night on the Mount of Olives. And the strength of these cross-
bearers helps Him after each of His falls.[13]

The righteous under the Old Covenant accompany Him on the
stretch of the way from the first to the second collapse. The disciples, both men and women, who surrounded Him during His
earthly life, assist Him on the second stretch.[14]

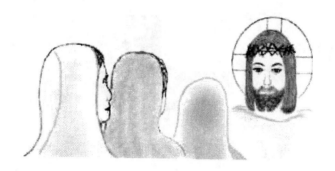

VIII
JESUS MEETS THE WOMEN OF JERUSALEM

Do not weep for Me. Weep for yourselves and for
your children (Luke 23:28).

The Savior today looks at us, solemnly probing us, and asks each
one of us: Will you remain faithful to the Crucified? Consider carefully! ... The battle between Christ and the Antichrist has broken
into the open. If you decide for Christ, it could cost you your life.[15]

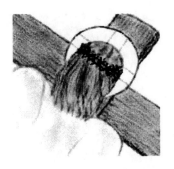

IX
JESUS FALLS A THIRD TIME

I looked about, but there was no one to help ...
no one to lend support (Is. 63:5).

The triple collapse under the burden of the cross corresponds to
the triple fall of humanity: the first sin; the rejection of the Savior
by His chosen people; the falling away of those who bear the
name of Christian.[16]

X
JESUS IS STRIPPED OF HIS GARMENTS

They divided His clothes among them
(Mt. 27:35).

The Savior hangs naked and destitute before you on the cross because He has chosen poverty ... . Gratefully receive what God's
providence sends you. Joyfully do without what He may let you
to do without.[17]

The denudation of the faculties that is demanded for this trans-
forming union is effected in the intellect through faith, in the memory through hope, and in the will through love ... The way that
leads to the high mountain of perfection can only be traveled by
those who are not weighed down by any burden. It is the way of
the cross to which the Lord invites His disciples.[18]

XI
JESUS IS NAILED TO THE CROSS

They have pierced my hands and feet
(Psalm 22:17).

Why did He choose the Lamb as the preferred symbol? ... . Because He was innocent as a lamb and meek as a lamb, and because He came in order to allow Himself to be led as a lamb to the slaughter [Is. 53:7] ... . The Lord permitted Himself to be bound at the Mount of Olives and nailed to the cross at Golgotha.[19]

Just as the Lamb had to be killed to be raised upon the throne of glory, so the path to glory leads through suffering and the cross for everyone chosen to attend the marriage supper of the Lamb. All who want to be married to the Lamb must allow themselves to be fastened to the cross with Him. Everyone marked by the blood of the Lamb is called to this, and that means all the baptized. But not everyone understands the call and follows it.[20]

XII
JESUS DIES ON THE CROSS

Through his suffering, my servant shall justify many
... he surrendered himself to death (Is. 53:11-12).

The Savior hangs before you with a pierced heart. He has spilled His heart's blood to win your heart ... . The arms of the Crucified are spread out to draw you to His heart. He wants your life in order to give you His.

Ave crux, spes unica![21]
[Hail, cross, our only hope!]

The cross is again raised before us. It is the sign of contradiction. The Crucified looks down on us: "Are you also going to abandon me?" ... The fountain from the heart of the Lamb has not dried up. We can wash our robes clean in it even today as the thief on Golgotha once did. Trusting in the atoning power of this holy fountain, we prostrate ourselves before the throne of the Lamb ... . Let us draw from the springs of salvation for ourselves and for the entire parched world.[22]

XIII
JESUS IS TAKEN DOWN FROM THE CROSS

They came and took the body away
(Jn. 19:38).

We already know from the Night of the Senses that a time arrives at
which all taste for spiritual exercises as well as for all terrestrial
things is taken away from the soul. She is put into total darkness and
emptiness. Absolutely nothing that might give her a hold is left to
her anymore except faith. Faith sets Christ before her eyes: the poor,
humiliated, crucified one, who is abandoned on the cross even by
His heavenly Father. In His poverty and abandonment she rediscov-
ers herself. Dryness, distaste, and affliction are the "purely spiritual
cross" that is handed to her. If she accepts it she experiences that
it is an easy yoke and a light burden. It becomes a staff for her that
will quickly lead her up the mountain. When she realizes that Christ,
in His extreme humiliation and annihilation on the cross, achieved
the greatest result, ... there awakens in her the understanding that
for her, also, annihilation, the "living death by crucifixion of all
that is sensory as well as spiritual" leads to union with God. Just
as Jesus in the extreme abandonment at His death surrendered
Himself into the hands of the invisible and incomprehensible
God, so will the soul yield herself to the midnight darkness of
faith which is the only way to the incomprehensible God.[23]

XIV
JESUS IS LAID IN THE TOMB

... but when they entered the tomb, they did not
find the body of the Lord Jesus (Luke 24:3).

The soul united with Christ lives out of His life — however, only
in surrender to the Crucified when she has traveled the entire way
of the cross with Him.[24]

Those who have a predilection for the way of the cross by no
means deny that Good Friday is past and that the work of salvation has been accomplished .... Only in union with the Divine Head
does human suffering take on expiatory power. To suffer and to be
happy although suffering, to have one's feet on the earth, to walk
on the dirty and rough paths of this earth and yet to be enthroned
with Christ at the Father's right hand, to laugh and cry with the
children of this world and ceaselessly sing the praises of God with
the choirs of angels — this is the life of the Christian until the
morning of eternity breaks forth.[25]

JESUS IS RISEN
ETERNAL LIFE:
UNION WITH THE HOLY TRINITY

In the Passion and death of Christ our sins were consumed by fire. If we accept that in faith, and if we accept the whole Christ in faith-filled surrender, which means, however, that we choose and walk the path of the imitation of Christ, then He will lead us "through His Passion and cross to the glory of His Resurrection." This is exactly what is experienced in contemplation: passing through the expiatory flames to the bliss of the union of love. This explains its twofold character. It is death and resurrection.[26]

The cross ... . It is the path from earth to heaven. It will lift one who embraces it in faith, love, and hope into the bosom of the Trinity.[27]

77

Notes

Quotations are from *The Collected Works of Edith Stein*, vol. 4, *The Hidden Life*, trans. Waltraut Stein (Washington, DC: ICS Publications, 1992); vol. 5, *Self-Portrait in Letters*, trans. Josephine Koeppel (Washington, DC: ICS Publications, 1993); vol. 6, *The Science of the Cross*, trans. Josephine Koeppel (Washington, DC: ICS Publications, 2002).

* Introductory quote: *The Science of the Cross*, by Edith Stein, ch. 21, p. 273.
1. *The Collected Works of Edith Stein: The Hidden Life*, vol. four, III.1, p. 92.
2. *Ibid.*
3. *Science*, ch. 23, p. 298.
4. *Hidden Life*, III.1, pp. 92-3.
5. *Collected Works: Self-Portrait in Letters*, vol. five, Letter 330, p. 341.
6. *Hidden Life*, III.1, pp. 91-2.
7. *Ibid.*, p. 92.
8. *Ibid.*, III.4, p. 104.
9. *Ibid.*, III.1, p. 92.
10. *Ibid.*, p. 91.
11. *Ibid.*, p. 92.
12. *Letters*, 281, p. 291.
13. *Hidden Life*, III.1, p. 92.
14. *Ibid.*
15. *Ibid.*, III.2, p. 94.
16. *Ibid.*, III.1, p. 92.
17. *Ibid.*, III.2, p. 95.
18. *Science*, ch. 4, pp. 61-62.
19. *Hidden Life*, III.3, p. 98.
20. *Ibid.*, p. 99.
21. *Ibid.*, III.2, p. 95.
22. *Ibid.*, III.3, p. 101.

23. *Science*, ch. 10, p. 121.
24. *Ibid.*, ch. 1, p. 20.
25. *Hidden Life*, III.1, p. 93.
26. *Science*, ch. 15, pp. 184-85.
27. *Hidden Life*, III.2, p. 95.

THE WAY OF THE CROSS
with Blessed Elizabeth of the Trinity

Cast all your anguish and concerns into His Heart. You can unite your agonies to His; He wanted to suffer first so that in crucifying hours we might be able to say, while looking at Him: "He has suffered even more than I, and did so in order to tell me of His love and to lay claim to mine."*

I
JESUS IS CONDEMNED TO DEATH

They all concurred in the verdict guilty, with its sentence of death (Mark 14:64).

May His holy will be the two-edged sword that immolates you at every moment; go learn this science near Jesus in the agony of the garden, when His crushed soul cried out: "May Your will be done and not mine" [Mk. 14:36].[1]

Then, when her hour of humiliation, of annihilation comes, she will recall this little phrase, "Jesus autem tacebat" ["But Jesus was silent" - Mt. 26:63]; and she will be silent, "keeping all her strength for the Lord" [cf. Ps. 58:10]; this strength which "we draw from silence" [cf. Is. 30:15]. And when the hour of abandonment, of desertion, and of anguish comes, the hour that drew from Christ this loud cry, "Why have You abandoned Me?" [Mt. 27:46], she will recall this prayer: "that they may have in themselves the fullness of My joy" [Jn. 17:13].[2]

II
JESUS CARRIES HIS CROSS

Jesus was led away ... carrying the cross
by Himself (John 19:16-17).

He loves you so much, and He has given you so many signs of it by asking you often, on your path of life, to help Him carry His cross.[3]

If despite everything, emptiness and sadness overwhelm you, unite this agony with that of the Master in the Garden of Olives, when He said to the Father: "If it is possible, let this cup pass Me by" [Mt. 26:39] ... . In the saddest times, think that the divine artist is using a chisel to make His work more beautiful, and remain at peace beneath the hand that is working on you.[4]

III
JESUS FALLS THE FIRST TIME

I was hard pressed and was falling
(Psalm 118:13).

And if I fall at every moment, in a wholly confident faith I will be helped up by Him. I know that He will forgive me, that He will cancel out everything with a jealous care, and even more, He will "despoil" me, He will "free" me [cf. Rom. 7:24] from all my miseries, from everything that is an obstacle to the divine action.[5]

IV
JESUS MEETS HIS AFFLICTED MOTHER

Simeon said to Mary His mother ... you yourself
shall be pierced with a sword (Luke 2:34-35).

This Queen of virgins is also Queen of martyrs; but again it was in
her heart that the sword pierced [cf. Lk. 2:35], for with her everything took place within ... Oh! How beautiful she is to contemplate during her long martyrdom, so serene, enveloped in a kind of
majesty that radiates both strength and gentleness .... She learned
from the Word Himself how those must suffer whom the Father
has chosen as victims, those whom He has decided to associate
with Himself in the great work of redemption, those whom He
"has foreknown and predestined to be conformed to His Christ"
[cf. Rom. 8:29], crucified by love.[6]

V

SIMON OF CYRENE HELPS JESUS
CARRY HIS CROSS

They pressed [Simon] into service to carry the
cross (Mark 15:21).

There is no wood like that of the cross for lighting the fire of love
in the soul! And Jesus needs to be loved and to find in the world,
where He is so offended, souls that are given, wholly surrendered
to Him and His good pleasure![7]

Let us lovingly eat this bread of the will of God. If sometimes
His will is more crucifying, we can doubtless say with our adored
Master: "Father, if it is possible, let this cup pass me by," but we will
add immediately: "Yet not as I will, but as you will" [Mt. 26:39];
and in strength and serenity, with the divine Crucified, we will
also climb our Calvary singing in the depths of our hearts and
raising a hymn of thanksgiving to the Father.[8]

VI
VERONICA WIPES THE FACE OF JESUS

**There was in Him no stately bearing to make us
look at Him (Is. 53:2).**

We will be glorified in the measure in which we will have been
conformed to the image of His divine Son [cf. Rom. 8: 29]. So let
us contemplate this adored Image, let us remain unceasingly under
its radiance so that it may imprint itself on us.[9]

He will communicate His power to you so you can love Him
with a love as strong as death [cf. Sg. 8:6]; the Word will imprint
in your soul, as in a crystal, the image of His own beauty, so you
may be pure with His purity, luminous with His light.[10]

VII
JESUS FALLS THE SECOND TIME

My strength has failed through affliction
(Psalm 31:11).

I have asked Him to make His home in me as Adorer, as Healer,
and as Savior, and I cannot tell you what peace it gives my soul
to think that He makes up for my weaknesses and, if I fall at
every passing moment, He is there to help me up again and carry
me further into Himself, into the depths of that divine essence
where we already live by grace and where I would like to bury
myself so deeply that nothing could make me leave.[11]

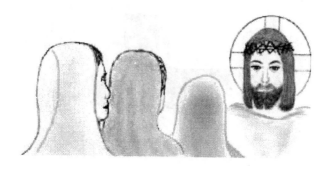

VIII
JESUS MEETS THE WOMEN OF JERUSALEM

Do not weep for Me. Weep for yourselves and for
your children (Luke 23:28).

So, when the divine Master finds a soul generous enough to share
His cross, He takes her as a partner in His suffering, and that soul
must accept it as a proof of the love of Him who wants her to be
like Him.[12]

"Because I love My Father, I do always the things that are
pleasing to Him" [Jn. 14:31; 8:25]. Thus spoke our holy Master,
and every soul who wants to live close to Him must also live this
maxim. ... It must let itself be immolated by all the Father's wishes in the likeness of His adored Christ. Each incident, each event,
each suffering, as well as each joy, is a sacrament which God
gives to it.[13]

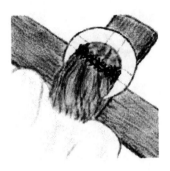

IX
JESUS FALLS A THIRD TIME

I looked about, but there was no one to help ... no
one to lend support (Is. 63:5).

"I die daily" [1 Cor. 15:31]. I decrease [cf. Jn. 3:30]. I renounce
self more each day so that Christ may increase in me and be
exalted ... I see "my nothingness, my misery, my weakness; I per-
ceive that I am incapable of progress, of perseverance; I see the
multitude of my shortcomings, my defects; I appear in my indi-
gence." "I fall down in my misery, confessing my distress, and I
display it before the mercy" of my Master.[14]

X
JESUS IS STRIPPED OF HIS GARMENTS

They divided His clothes among them
(Mt. 27:35).

"Strip off the old man in whom you lived your former life," ...
"and put on the new man, who has been created according to God
in justice and holiness" [Eph. 4:22, 24]. This is the way set forth;
we have only to strip off self to follow it as God wills! To strip
off self, to die to self, to lose sight of self. It seems to me the
Master meant this when He said: "If anyone wants to follow Me,
let him take up his cross and deny himself [cf. Mt. 16:24]. ... "O
death," says the Lord, "I will be your death" [Ho. 13:14]; that is,
O soul, ... look at Me and you will forget yourself; ... come die
in Me that I may live in you![15]

The soul thus "stripped" of self and "clothed" in Jesus Christ
[cf. Col. 3:9-10; Gal. 3:27] has nothing more to fear from exterior
encounters or from interior difficulties, for these things, far from
being an obstacle, save only "to root it more deeply in the love"
[Eph. 3:17] of its Master. Through everything, despite everything,
the soul can "adore Him always because of Himself" [Ps. 71:15].
For it is free, rid of self and everything else.[16]

XI
JESUS IS NAILED TO THE CROSS

They have pierced my hands and feet
(Psalm 22:17).

I believe that the secret of peace and happiness is to forget oneself,
not be preoccupied with oneself. That doesn't mean not feeling
one's physical or mental sufferings; the saints themselves passed
through these crucifying states. But they did not dwell on them;
they continually left these things behind them … . Try then to will
to be wholly joyful under the hand that crucifies you; I would
even say that you should look at each suffering, each trial, "as a
proof of love" that comes to you directly from God in order to
unite you to Him.[17]

[God's] will, at times so crucifying, never ceases to be all love,
since love is the very essence of God.[18]

XII
JESUS DIES ON THE CROSS

Through his suffering, my servant shall justify
many ... he surrendered himself to death
(Is. 53:11-12).

Rejoice in the thought that from all eternity we have been known by the Father, as St. Paul says, and that He wishes to find once again in us the image of His crucified Son [cf. Rom. 8:29]. Oh, if you knew how necessary suffering is so God's work can be done in the soul … . God has an immense desire to enrich us with His graces, but it is we who determine the amount to the extent that we know how to let ourselves be immolated by Him, immolated in joy, in thanksgiving, like the Master, saying with Him: "Am I not to drink the cup my Father has prepared for me?" [Jn. 18:11] The Master called the hour of His passion "His hour" [Jn. 12:27], the one He had come for, the one He invoked with all His desire! When a great suffering or some very little sacrifice is offered us, oh, let us think very quickly that "this is our Hour," the hour when we are going to prove our love for Him who has "loved us exceedingly" … [cf. Eph. 2:4].[19]

Do not forget that love, to be true, must be sacrificed: "He loved me, He gave Himself for me" [Gal. 2:20], there is the culmination of love.[20]

XIII
JESUS IS TAKEN DOWN FROM THE CROSS

They came and took the body away
(Jn. 19:38).

She is there at the foot of the cross, standing, full of strength and courage, and here my Master says to me: "Ecce Mater tua" ["Behold your Mother" - Jn. 19:27]. He gives her to me for my Mother ... . And now that He has returned to the Father and has substituted me for Himself on the cross so that "I may suffer in my body what is lacking in His passion for the sake of His body, which is the Church" [Col. 1:24], the Blessed Virgin is again there to teach me to suffer as He did.[21]

Let us live by love so we may die of love and glorify the God who is all love.[22]

XIV
JESUS IS LAID IN THE TOMB

... but when they entered the tomb, they did not
find the body of the Lord Jesus (Luke 24:3).

"Let us believe in love" with Saint John [1 Jn. 4:16], and, since we possess Him within us, what does it matter if nights obscure our heaven: if Jesus seems to be asleep, oh, let us rest near Him; let us be very calm and silent; let us not wake Him but wait in faith.[23]

It is by the Blood of the cross that He will make peace in my little heaven, so that it may truly be the repose of the Three. He will fill me with Himself; He will bury me with Him; He will make me live again with Him, by His life.[24]

O my Three, ... I surrender myself to You as Your prey. Bury Yourself in me that I may bury myself in You until I depart to contemplate in Your light the abyss of Your greatness.[25]

JESUS IS RISEN
ETERNAL LIFE:
UNION WITH THE HOLY TRINITY

There are two words that sum up for me all holiness, all apostolate: "Union and Love." Ask that I may live that fully, and, for that purpose, dwell completely hidden away in the Holy Trinity.[26]

"Silence is Your praise!" [Ps. 65:1] Yes, this is the most beautiful praise since it is sung eternally in the bosom of the tranquil Trinity; and it is also the "last effort of the soul that overflows and can say no more." [Lacordaire][27]

Notes

Quotations are from *The Complete Works of Elizabeth of the Trinity*, vol. 1, *General Introduction Major Spiritual Writings*, trans. Aletheia Kane (ICS Publications, 1984); vol. 2, *Letters from Carmel*, trans. Anne Englund Nash (Washington, DC: ICS Publications, 1995).

* Introductory quote: *The Complete Works*, vol. two, L263 – to Madame de Sourdon, p. 248.
1. *Complete Works*, vol. two, L291 – to Louise Demoulin, p. 294.
2. *Ibid.*, vol. one, *Last Retreat*, 14th day, no. 39, p. 159.
3. *Ibid.*, vol. two, L280 – to her mother, p. 280.
4. *Ibid.*, L248 – to Madame Angles, p. 230.
5. Ibid., vol. one, *Last Retreat*, 12th day, no. 31, p. 156.
6. *Ibid.*, *Last Retreat*, 15th day, no. 41, pp. 160-61.
7. *Ibid.*, vol. two, L138 – to Madame Angles, p. 68.
8. *Ibid.*, vol. one, *Heaven in Faith*, 8th day, no. 30, pp. 106-07.
9. *Ibid.*, *Heaven in Faith*, 8th day, no. 27, p. 105.
10. *Ibid.*, vol. two, L269 – to her sister, p. 265.
11. *Ibid.*, L214 – to Abbé Chevignard, p. 179.
12. *Ibid.*, L258 – to her Rolland aunts, p. 242.
13. *Ibid.*, vol. one, *Heaven In Faith*, 3rd day, no. 10, p. 97.
14. *Ibid.*, *Heaven in Faith*, 3rd day, no. 12, p. 97.
15. *Ibid.*, *Last Retreat*, 9th day, no. 24, p. 152.
16. *Ibid.*, *Last Retreat*, 13th day, no. 33, p. 157.
17. *Ibid.*, vol. two, L249 – to Madame Angles, pp. 228-29.
18. *Ibid.*, L257 – to Madame d'Anthès, p. 241.
19. *Ibid.*, L308 – to her mother, p. 322.
20. *Ibid.*, L278 – to Germaine de Geneaux, p. 278.
21. *Ibid.*, vol. one, *Last Retreat*, 15th day, no. 41, p. 161.
22. *Ibid.*, vol. two, L335 – to Sister Marie-Odile, p. 360.
23. *Ibid.*, L239 – to her sister, p. 216.
24. *Ibid.*, vol. one, *Last Retreat*, 12th day, no. 31, p. 156.
25. *Ibid.*, O My God, Trinity Whom I Adore, p. 164.
26. *Ibid.*, vol. two, L191 – to Abbé Chevignard, p. 145.
27. *Ibid.*, vol. one, *Last Retreat*, 8th day, no. 21, p. 150.

The Institute of Carmelite Studies promotes research and publication in the field of Carmelite spirituality. Its members are Discalced Carmelites, part of a Roman Catholic community — friars, nuns and laity — who are heirs to the teaching and way of life of Teresa of Jesus and John of the Cross; men and women dedicated to contemplation and to ministry in the Church and the world. Information concerning their way of life is available through local diocesan Vocation Offices or from the Vocation Directors' Offices:

2131 Lincoln Road, NE, Washington, DC 20002

P. O. Box 3420, San Jose, CA 95156-3420

4600 West Davis, Dallas, TX 75211